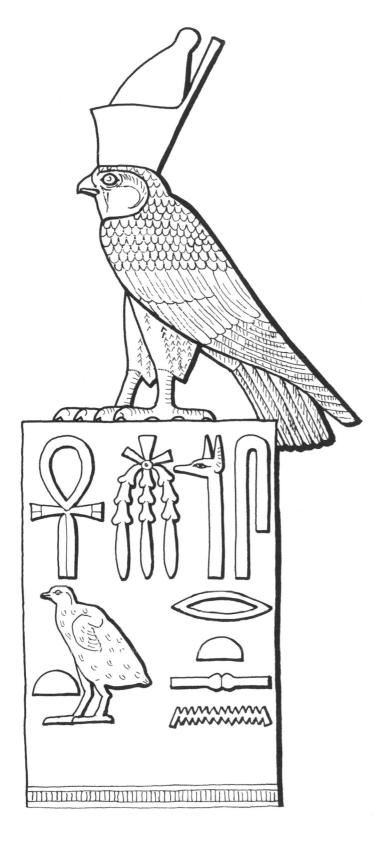

3 In ancient Egypt the king was seen as a god. Here, the falcon god Horus protects the king's name and the god of the Nile brings him offerings.

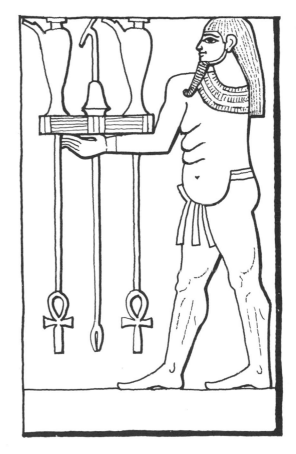

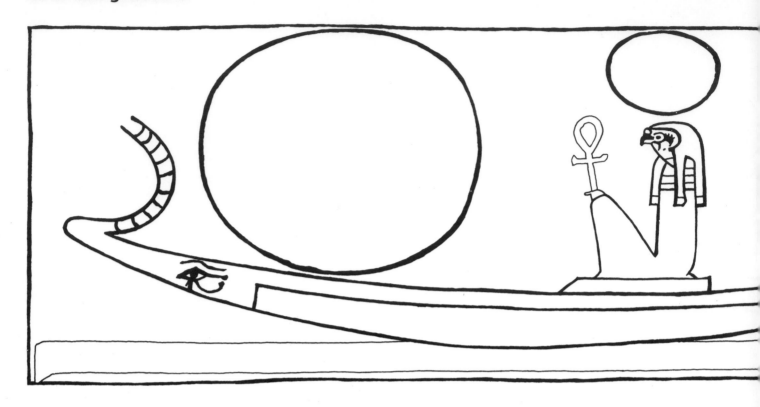

4 The Egyptians believed that the sun god Re crossed the sky in a boat every day.

1. Religion was very important to the ancient Egyptians. This priest is offering food and vases of water to the falcon-headed god Ra-Horakhty.

**Gods and goddesses**

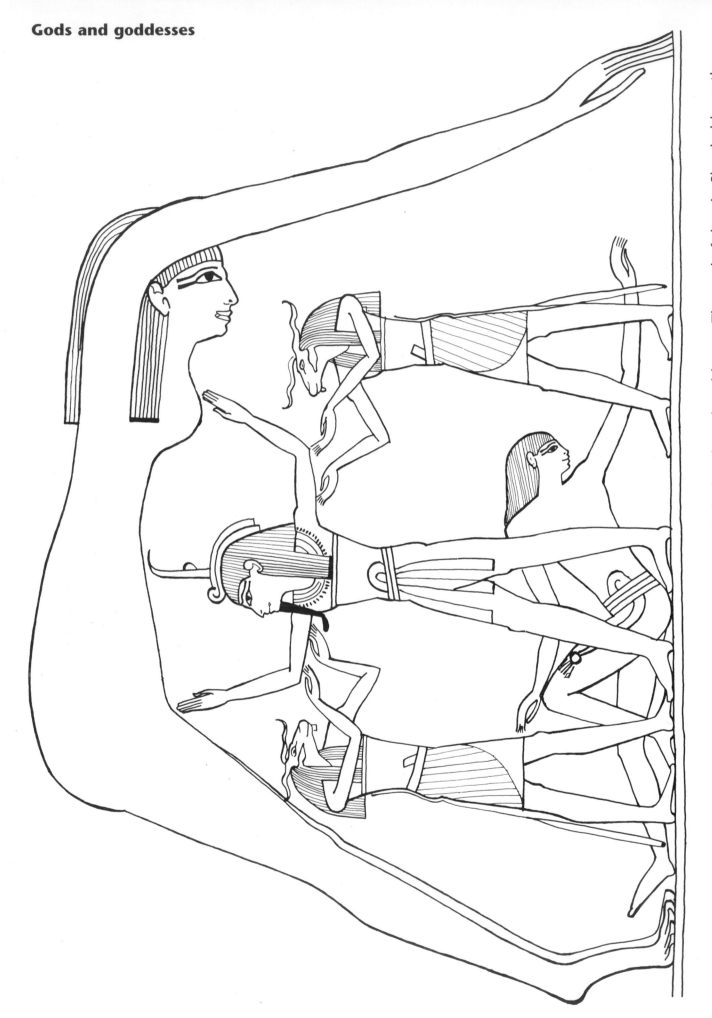

2. The ancient Egyptians believed that the earth and sky were full of gods and goddesses. The god of the air, Shu, holds up the sky goddess, Nut. The earth god (lying down) is Geb.

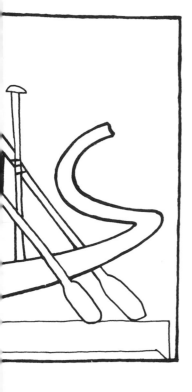

5 At night, the boat of Re sailed through the underworld.

6 The god of the dead, Osiris, and Maat the goddess of truth.

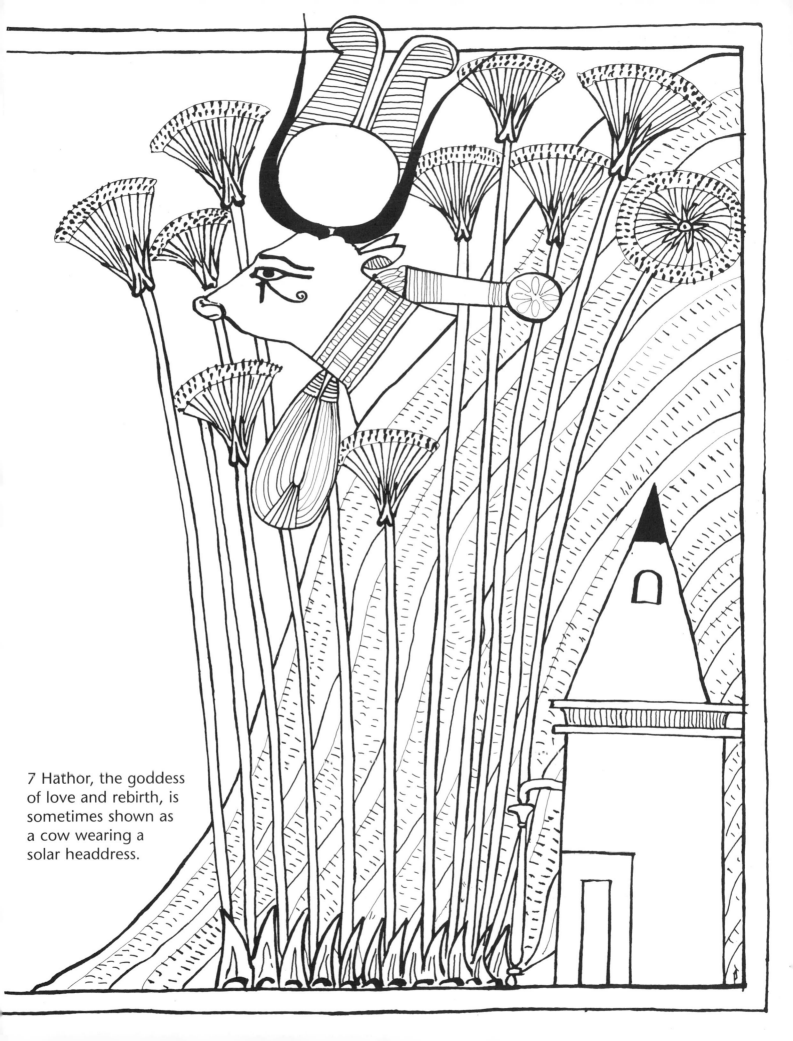

7 Hathor, the goddess
of love and rebirth, is
sometimes shown as
a cow wearing a
solar headdress.

8 Egyptian mummies wore beautiful masks. This one belonged to a princess called Satdjehuty.

9 This mummy mask was made for a priest called Hornedjitef.

10 This is the mummy mask of a lady called Henutmehit.

11 A funeral. The man's wife is weeping and the god of the dead, Anubis, is taking care of his mummified body.

12 The Egyptians believed that when a person died their heart was weighed in the scales opposite the goddess of Truth to prove that he or she had been good during their lifetime.

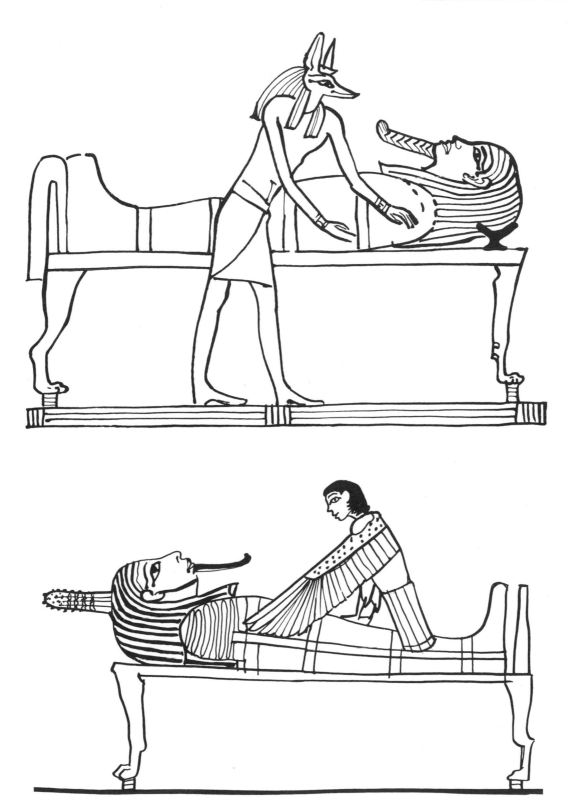

13 A priest wearing the mask of Anubis prepares a mummy. The soul of the dead man, in the shape of a human-headed bird, sits on his mummy.

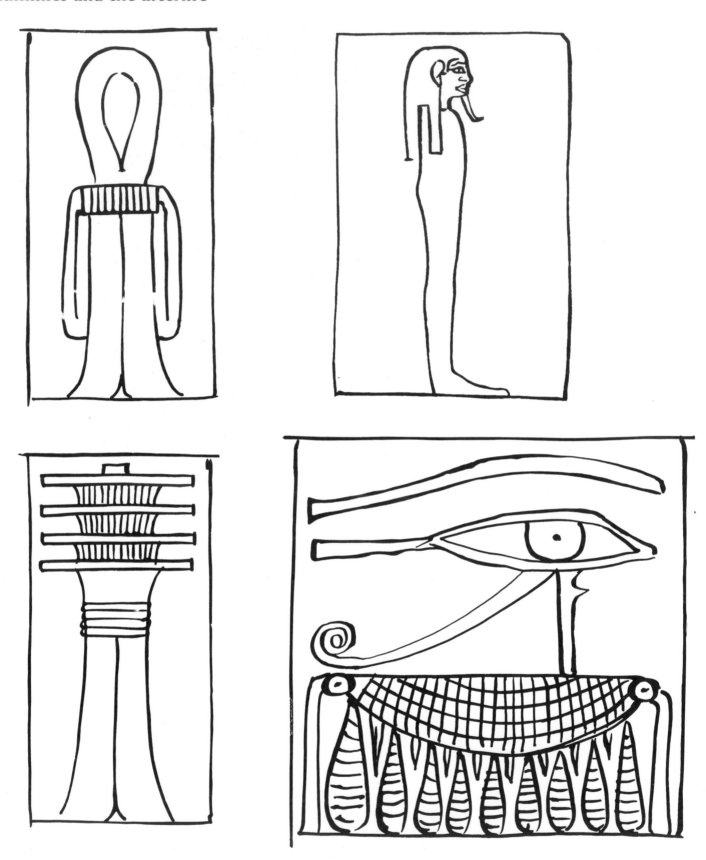

14 Mummies were given special amulets to protect them. These are the djed pillar of Osiris, the knot of Isis, a shabti figure and the Eye of Horus.

15 The king, or pharaoh, was the most important person in ancient Egypt, almost a god.

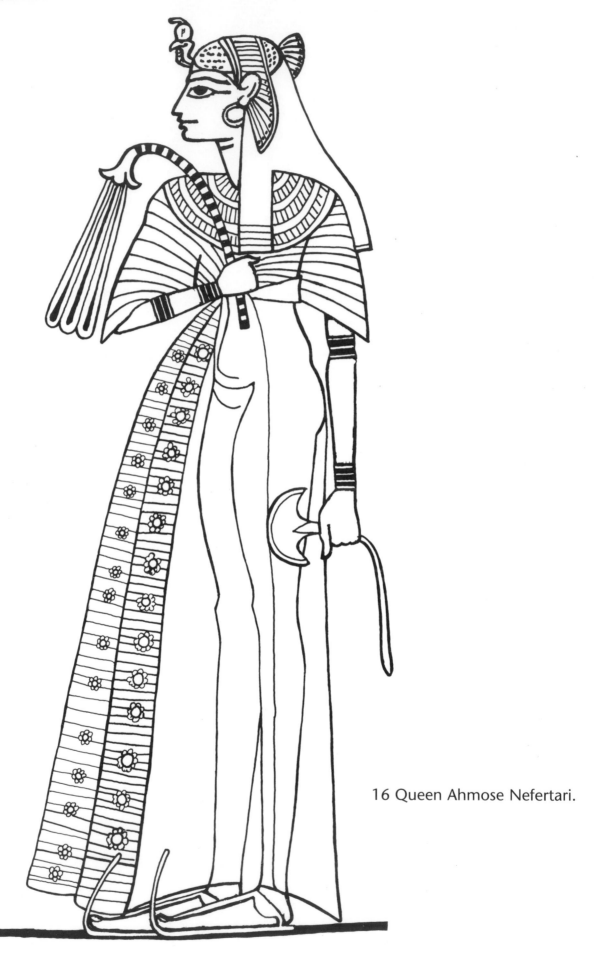

16 Queen Ahmose Nefertari.

17 King Rameses the Great captures an enemy in war.

18 An Egyptian house

19 A man and woman in their garden, which has a pool surrounded by trees.

20 This picture of a father, mother and two children was carved on a tomb.
The children's names are written in hieroglyphs: Neferhotephathor and Nisuredy.

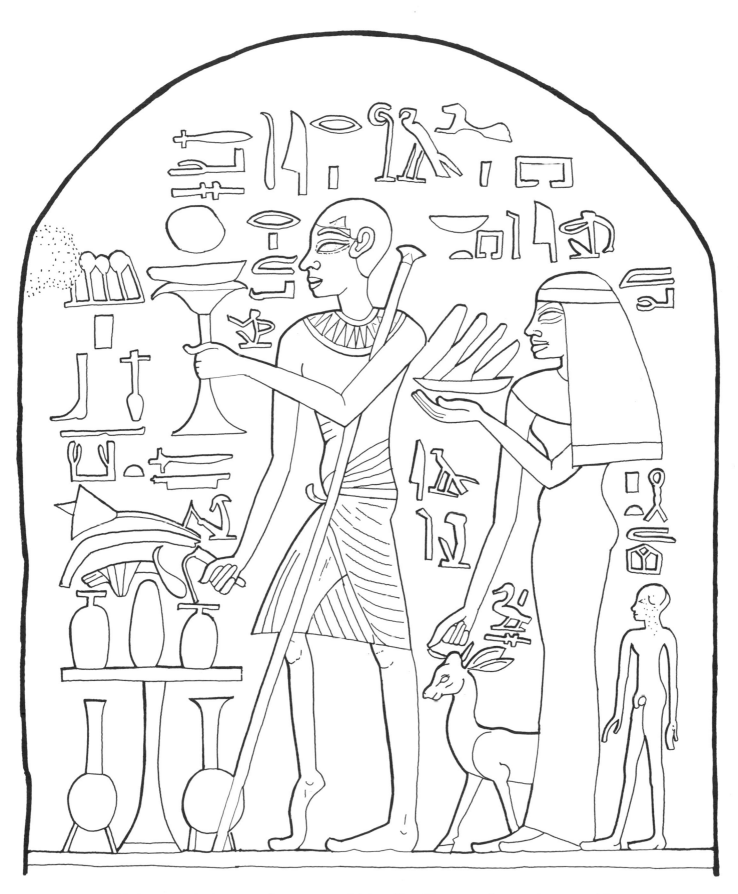

21 A carved picture of a man and his wife. The man has a damaged leg
and carries a stick to help him walk.

22 Ity and his wife are given food by their two sons, Intef and Amenemhat.
Below two of Ity's daughters are smelling lotus flowers.

23 Guests at a feast are given wine by a serving girl.

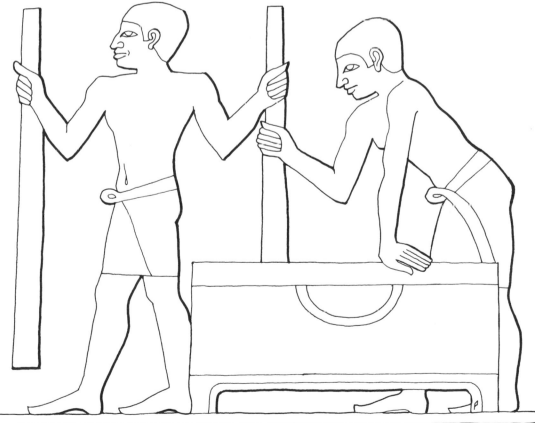

24 Rich Egyptians had servants to work for them. In the top picture a servant is driving donkeys towards a scribe, who is writing down how many donkeys there are. Below, two servants are making a bed, while others bring clean sheets. The bed has a wooden headrest instead of a pillow.

25 An artist painting.

26 Two sailing boats. The River Nile was an important means of transport in ancient Egypt.

27 The farmer in the top picture is cutting corn with a sickle. In the bottom picture he is ploughing with oxen.

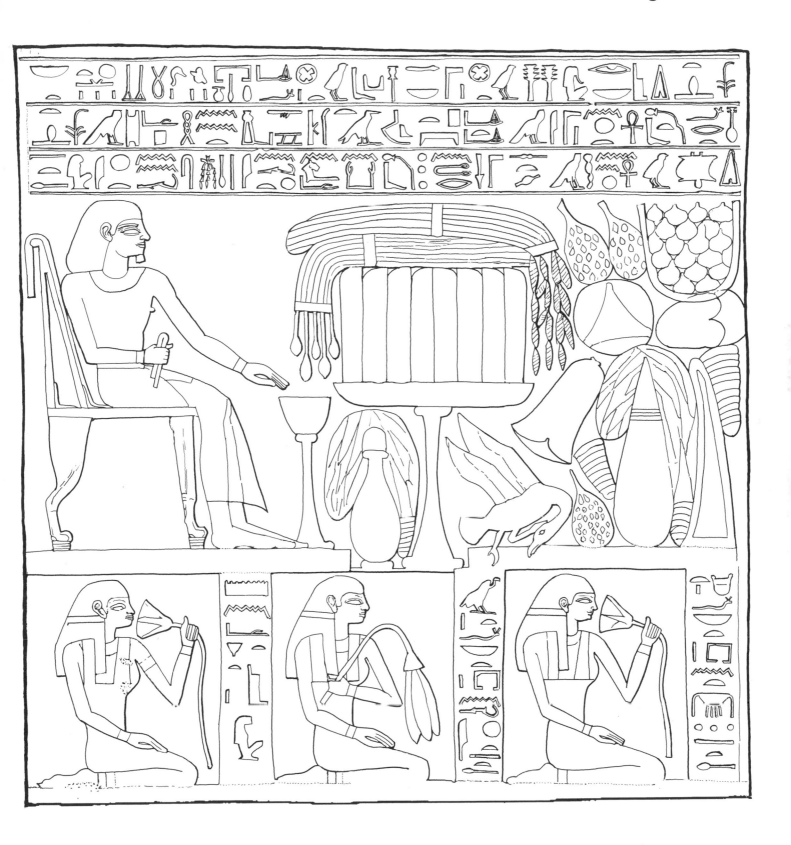

28 A carving from a stela. Nakht has a pile of food to last him all eternity. It includes beef, vegetables, fruit and a duck. Below sit a row of his female relatives, including his wife and mother.

29 Some Egyptian animals.

30 Some dangerous animals
from ancient Egypt.

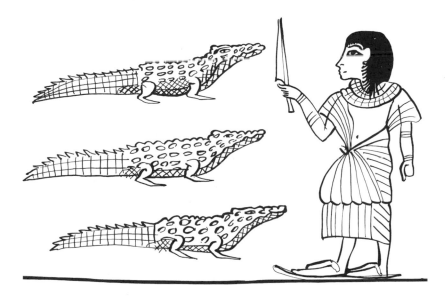

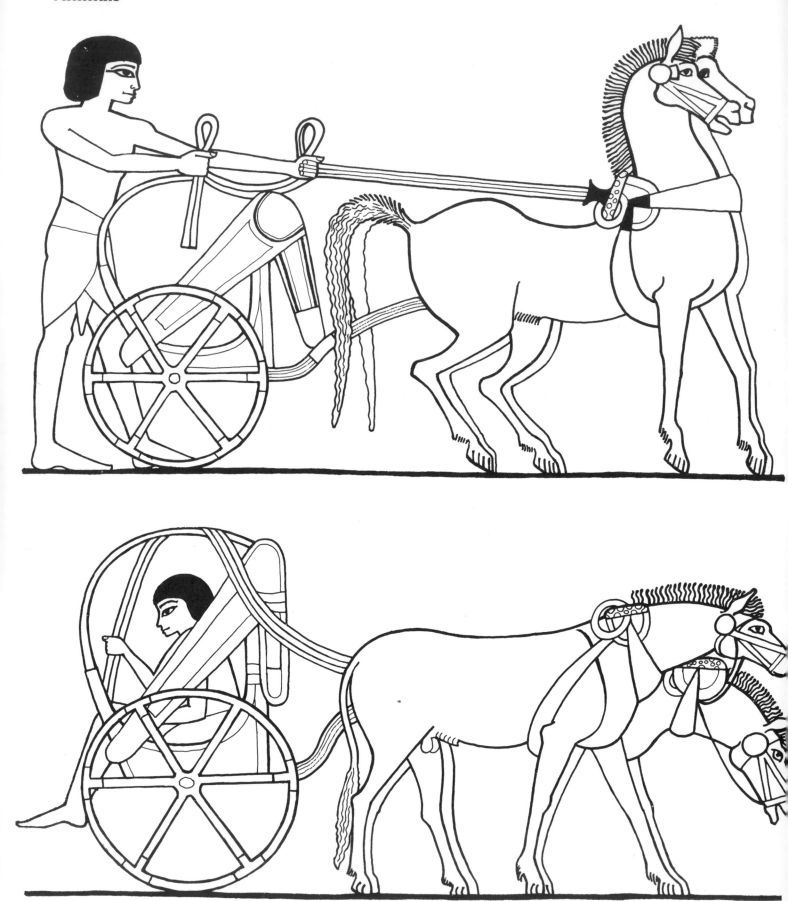

31 The ancient Egyptians used horses and mules to pull their chariots.

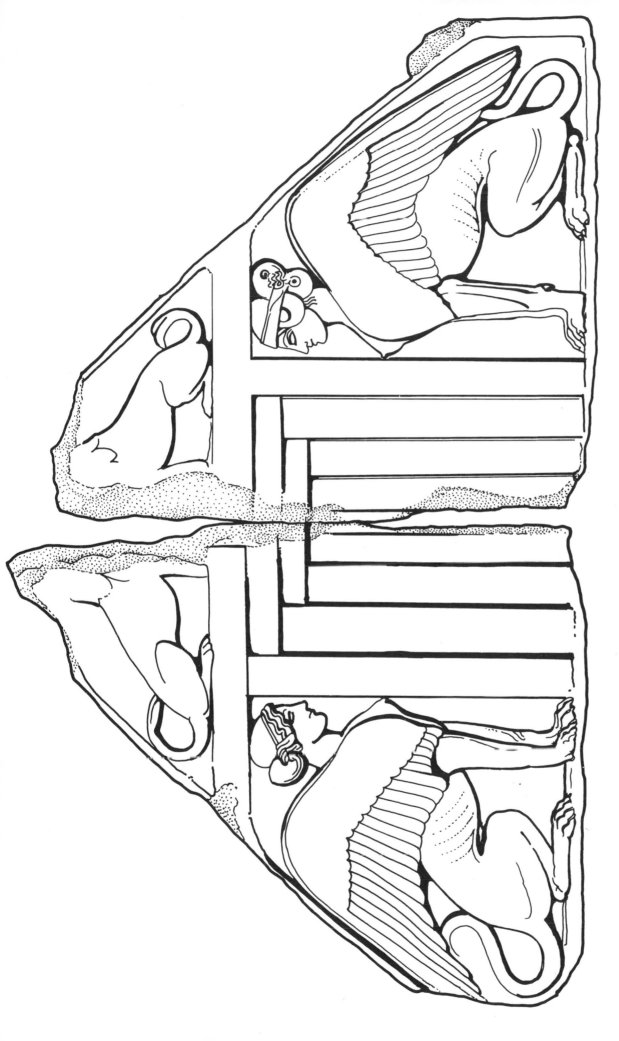

32 Sphinxes have the body of a lion with a human head. The most famous Sphinx is at Giza in Egypt, but these two are carved on a tomb in Greece.

33 Sometimes the Egyptians painted animals in a comical way, doing human things. Cats are acting as servants to a mouse lady, and hyenas are looking after an ox.

34 (left) This lion and antelope are playing a board game called senet. The lion looks as if he is winning.

# Egyptian writing

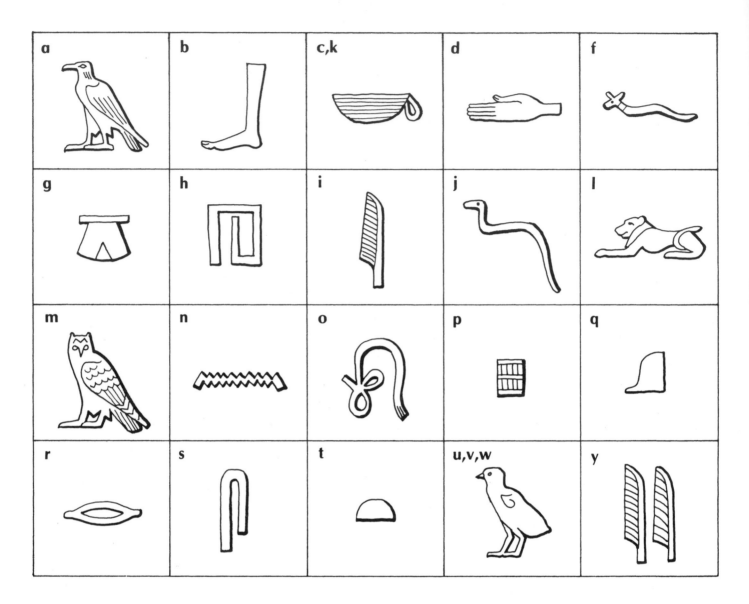

35 An 'alphabet' of Egyptian hieroglyphs. The loop at the bottom is called a 'cartouche'. Important royal names were written inside cartouches.

36 The hieroglyphs around this picture are like a
speech bubble. The man cooking is saying, "I have
been roasting since the beginning of time.
I have never seen the like of this goose."

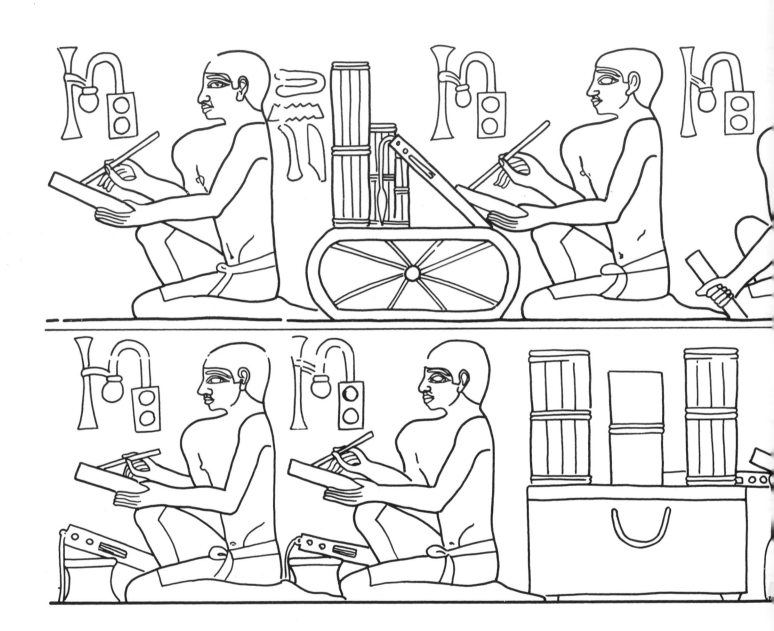

37 Egyptian scribes at work.

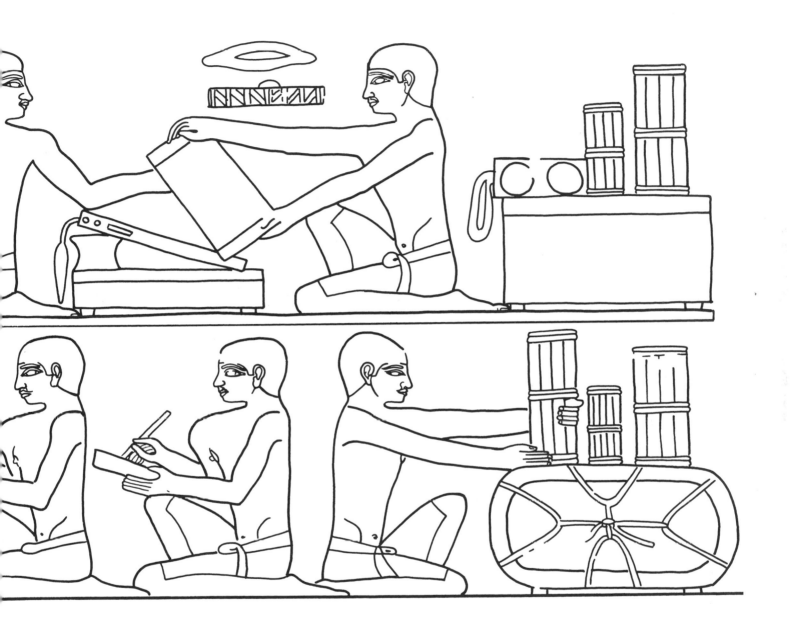

38 The Assyrians were powerful enemies of Egypt. This is the Assyrian king Ashurbanipal in his chariot, preparing to go out hunting.

39 The Assyrian king Shalmaneser III receiving tribute. The camels at the bottom are tribute from Egypt.

40 An Egyptian vase showing two Philistine captives.

41 Egypt was invaded by the Persians twice. These are two Persian soldiers.

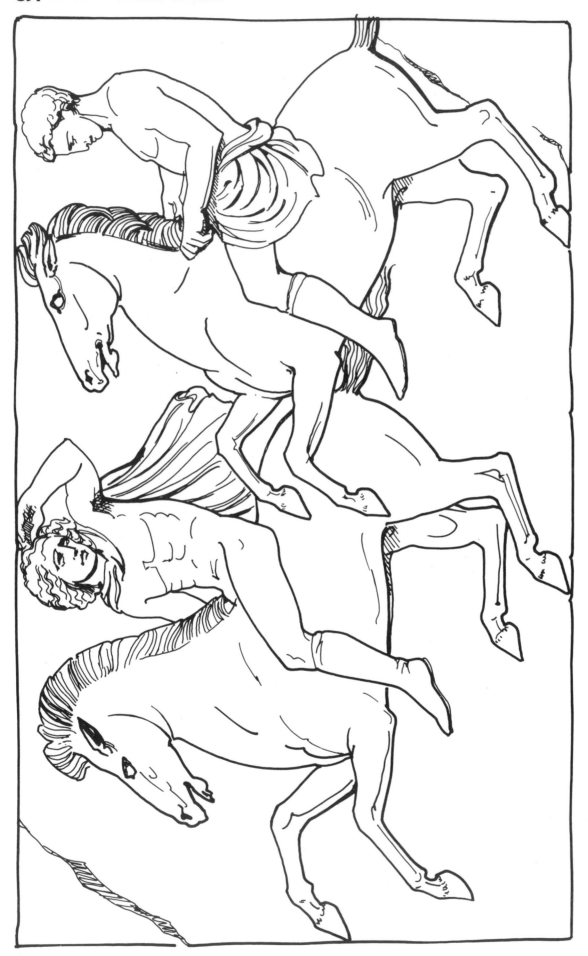

42 Egypt was ruled by Greek kings from 332 BC. These young Greek horsemen are carved on the Parthenon frieze from Athens.

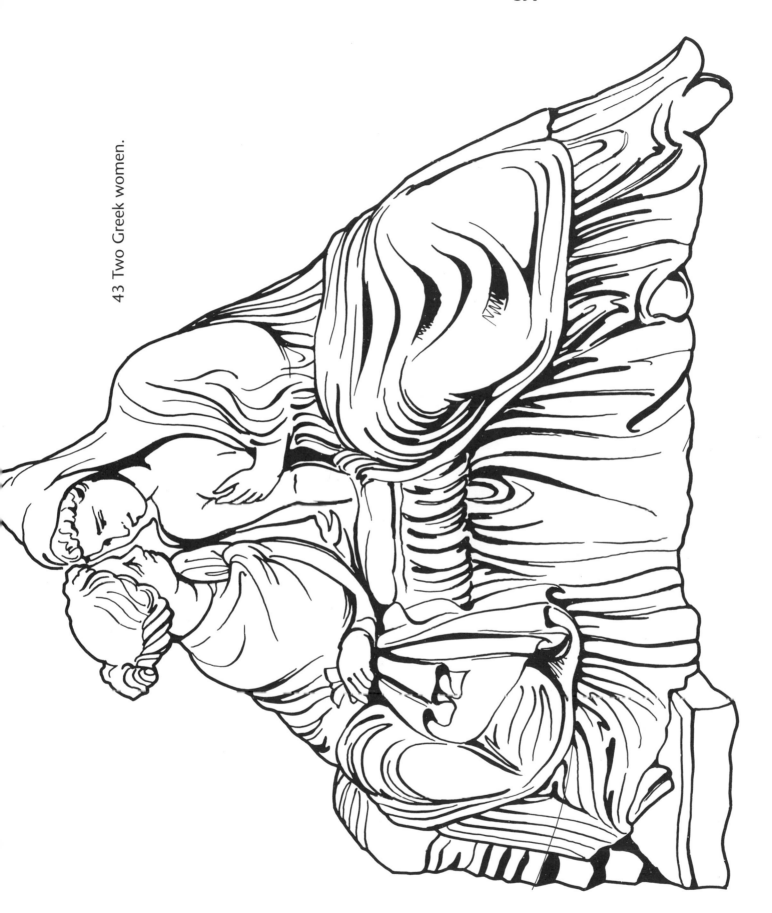

43 Two Greek women.

44 A Roman soldier.

45 A wealthy Roman family having dinner. Egypt was ruled by Rome
for over 400 years and adopted Roman customs.

46 The Roman emperor Augustus, who conquered Egypt in 30 BC.

© 2004 The Trustees of the British Museum

Published in 2004 by British Museum Press
A division of The British Museum Company Ltd
46 Bloomsbury Street, London WC1B 3QQ

ISBN 0 7141 3100 8
A catalogue record for this title is available from the British Library

Front cover illustration by Claire Thorne.
Designed and typeset by Martin Richards.
Printed in Hong Kong.

*The illustrations were drawn by:*

Richard Parkinson, Department of Ancient Egypt and Sudan, British Museum: 1, 2, 3, 4, 5, 6, 7, 11, 12, 15, 16, 17, 20, 21, 22, 23, 24, 25, 27, 28, 31, 33, 34, 35, 37

Claire Thorne, Department of Ancient Egypt and Sudan, British Museum: 13, 14, 18, 19, 26, 29, 30, 36

John Green: 8, 9, 10, 44, 45, 46

Sue Bird: 32, 42, 43

Patricia Hansom: 38, 39, 40, 41